EXTREME SURVIVAL

SURVIVING STUNTS AND OTHER AMAZING FEATS

Patrick Catel

Chicago, Illinois

www.heinemannraintree.com
Visit our website to find out
more information about
Heinemann-Raintree books.

To order:

☎ Phone 888-454-2279

🖥 Visit www.heinemannraintree.com
to browse our catalog and order online.

Edited by Adam Miller, Adrian Vigliano, and Andrew
Farrow
Designed by Steve Mead
Original illustrations © Capstone Global Library Ltd.
Picture research by Tracy Cummins
Production by Camilla Crask
Originated by Capstone Global Library Ltd
Printed and bound in the United States of America,
North Mankato, MN

15 14 13 12 11
10 9 8 7 6 5 4 3 2 1

Library of Congress Cataloging-in-Publication Data
Catel, Patrick.
  Extreme survival : surviving stunts and other
amazing feats / Patrick Catel.
      p. cm.
  Includes bibliographical references and index.
  ISBN 978-1-4109-3969-2 (hc)
  ISBN 978-1-4109-3976-0 (pb)
  1. Daredevils. 2. Survival skills. I.Title.
  GV1839.C38 2011
  613.6´9—dc22   2010028690

Acknowledgments
The author and publishers are grateful to the
following for permission to reproduce copyright
material: AP Photo p. **44** (The Plain Deale/David
I. Andersen); Corbis pp. **48** (©HO/Reuters),
5 (©Hulton-Deutsch Collection), **29** (©Lech
Muszyñski/PAP), **27** (©Pilar Olivares/Reuters),
38 (©Rick Doyle), **6** (©Tom Fox/Dallas Morning
News), **25** (©Toru Hanai/Reuters); Getty Images
pp. **7** (Adam Clark), **8 & 9** (AFP), **37** (Ahmad Yusni/
AFP Photo), **33** (Buyenlarge/Time Life Pictures), **13**
(Christopher Furlong), **47** (Emmanuel Aguirre), **42**
(Jim Bourg), **39** (JUNG YEON-JE/Staff), **43** (Mahaux
Photography), **35** (Michael Bradley), **40 & 41** (Mike
Blabac/Quiksilver/DC), **26** (SAM PANTHAKY/
AFP), **28** (STR/AFP), **19** (Venturelli/WireImage);
Library of Congress pp. **32, 34**; Rex Features p. **16**
(©Niles Jorgensen); Shutterstock pp. **15** (©Birute
Vijeikiene), **31** (©Brooke Whatnall), **49** (©Darren
Brode), **46** (©kojoku); THE KOBAL COLLECTION pp.
21 (20TH CENTURY FOX), **22** (ROGUE PICTURES);
ZUMA Press p. **10** (©Fu Xin/ChinaFotoPress).

Cover photograph of daredevil performing a stunt
reproduced with the permission of Getty Images/
Kaushik Roy/India.

We would like to thank Ann Fullick for her invaluable
help in the preparation of this book.

Every effort has been made to contact copyright
holders of any material reproduced in this book. Any
omissions will be rectified in subsequent printings if
notice is given to the publisher.

CONTENTS

Some words are printed in bold, **like this**. You can find out what they mean by looking in the glossary.

ADVENTURE AND AMAZEMENT

How far can a person jump, fall, fly, swim, or run? How strong or fast can a person be? Some people have a desire to test these limits in strange—and often dangerous—ways.

There is the idea of the human cannonball, for instance. It takes a unique person to want to be shot out of a cannon! Some people play with other kinds of danger. The art of sword-swallowing has been practiced for hundreds, or even thousands, of years. If swallowing swords seems amazing, how about eating and breathing fire? Or walking on hot coals? And who would want to voluntarily set themselves on fire for a job? Stunt people deal with fire all the time to make movie magic.

People who like to do dangerous things are sometimes called daredevils. Daredevils have tried many dangerous stunts throughout history. They often risk serious injury—or even death. Sometimes they do this as a test of their own abilities or to break a record. Other daredevils perform dangerous feats in order to entertain an audience.

THE AMAZING ZAZEL

Rosa Richter, using the stage name "Zazel," became the first human cannonball on April 2, 1877, in London, England, when she was just 14 years old. She was shot about 21 meters (70 feet) into the air. Zazel later performed in the P. T. Barnum Circus, beginning a long tradition of human cannonballs.

The human cannonball stunt uses a giant spring or jet of compressed air to shoot a person into the air. Gunpowder is used simply to provide special effects.

Limits of body and mind

Some daredevils defy the limits of human strength by pulling things like trucks and trains with only their muscles. Others test human endurance—or the ability to keep pushing through challenges—in record journeys across land and sea. For instance, in 1998 French swimmer Benoit Lecomte swam across the Atlantic Ocean!

Other people challenge the limits of the mind. For example, some people claim to practice the art of levitation (floating), while others claim they can move things with their minds. Do you think these feats are possible? The martial arts, or fighting arts, test the limits of both mind and body. Some of the dangerous feats martial artists accomplish seem to defy explanation.

Humans and machines

Humans have invented machines such as motorcycles, cars, and airplanes that allow us to travel faster and farther than ever before. Daredevils use those machines to push their limits with ever-wilder stunts. Imagine the rush a person might get from driving a fast motorcycle. Now, imagine what it might feel like to jump a motorcycle across the huge gap of a canyon!

Daredevil Robbie Knieval hurtles over 21 SUVs parked side-by-side. He performed this stunt in Texas in 2008.

As you will see in this book, human beings are always finding new ways to push their bodies—and their performances—to the limit. Read on to learn more about some amazing stunts and feats.

THE ADRENALINE RUSH

Some people crave the thrill of more adventurous, dangerous, and even life-threatening stunts and feats. Sometimes they risk their lives in search of a record, a thrill, or even just a rush of **adrenaline**. Adrenaline is a chemical produced in the body when a person is excited by fear or anger. It makes the heart beat faster and briefly improves the body's ability to deal with a stressful situation.

A WORD OF WARNING

The stunts and feats you will read about are not normal, easy accomplishments. The people involved have years of training and are experts at what they do. Benoit Lecomte, for instance, was only able to swim an ocean after two years of training and the help of many experts. Even trained experts are often seriously injured, and some even die. DO NOT TRY THESE STUNTS!

SIDESHOW ARTS

Throughout history, traveling circuses, carnivals, and fairs have offered a variety of daring entertainers, such as sword-swallowers, fire-eaters, and more. These stunts and feats are often called "sideshows," and they have inspired the performers to push their physical and mental limits. They also give audiences incredible thrills!

Living by the sword

Fencing and swordplay are fun in the movies, but real swords have sharp, steel blades, and can seriously harm or kill people. Knowing that, why would someone try to swallow one? Or even several? Despite the danger, people have been performing sword-swallowing stunts for hundreds, or even thousands, of years, beginning in ancient India.

Don't try this at home!

Today, Indian-born Natasha Veruschka calls herself the world's only belly-dancing sword-swallower. She holds seven sword-swallowing world records. Natasha swallows the "Neon Sword" as part of her act. The sword is glass and filled with poisonous gas. It is fragile enough that a person's stomach muscles could shatter it while the sword is being swallowed. It is also electric and gets hot. If it gets too hot, it could stick to the swallower's insides.

Natasha came very close to death one time, when a man pushed her while she had three swords inside her. The blades cut her lower **esophagus** (see the box on page 11). She lost a dangerous amount of blood and almost died.

Sword-swallowing is extremely dangerous and requires a great deal of training. There are probably only a few hundred people in the world who can safely perform these amazing feats.

9

"The Space Cowboy"

There have been many other daring sword-swallowers. On March 28, 2008, an Australian man named Chayne Hultgren, also known as "The Space Cowboy," set the record of 17 swords swallowed at one time. Chayne also holds the Guinness World Record for the heaviest weight dangled from a swallowed sword: he held 22.4 kilograms (49 pounds, 6 ounces) for five seconds.

The art of sword-swallowing

But what, exactly, are these daredevils doing? Sword-swallowing involves putting a sword in the mouth and passing it down the esophagus toward the stomach, and sometimes even into the stomach. The esophagus is the tube that connects the back of the throat to the stomach. The handle of the sword remains outside the mouth, and the sword is eventually carefully removed. (Read the box at right to understand how sword-swallowers force their bodies to go against their natural instincts.)

This Chinese folk performer is demonstrating a unique sword-swallowing routine. Sword-swallowing has been practiced in China for many decades.

SURVIVAL SCIENCE

The science behind sword-swallowing

Sword-swallowing does not involve actual swallowing. In fact, it requires the "swallower" to repress, or hold back, the act of swallowing. This keeps the passage to the stomach open. You are probably familiar with the **gag reflex**. The human body is built to gag to prevent foreign objects from going down the throat. Sword-swallowers must learn to overcome the gag reflex.

To achieve this, their bodies must be totally relaxed. The physical position of the body is also very important. Sword-swallowers lean their head back and extend their neck. Swallowers then relax a **sphincter** muscle, which would otherwise act on its own to close the top of the esophagus.

Once the sword passes the pharynx and sphincter, it straightens out the esophagus, which is flexible. Sometimes, the blade is actually slipped down into the stomach. The stomach is located at an angle to the esophagus. However, as the sword enters, the stomach is brought into line with the straightened esophagus. The sword can only be kept down for a few seconds, because it is very difficult to hold back the gag reflex.

Sword-swallowing is extremely dangerous. The swords pass within millimeters of vital blood vessels and organs.

1. The sword enters the mouth.

2. The sword passes down the throat.

3. The sword passes through the upper esophageal sphincter, which must be relaxed.

4. The sword passes through the esophagus, which straightens as the sword enters.

5. The sword passes through the lower esophageal sphincter, which must be relaxed.

6. The sword enters the stomach.

Breathing fire

Fire-breathing is another popular feat often seen in carnivals and circuses. Fire-breathers create the **illusion** of "breathing" fire by exhaling large bursts of flame. How do they do it? As you might guess, there is a trick to this amazing feat (see box below). However, the danger to the fire-breather is very real.

SURVIVAL SCIENCE

The science of breathing fire

The science behind the feat of fire-breathing is fairly simple. The person projects a fine mist of fuel over an open flame. The mist of fuel ignites, creating a large plume of fire. The fire-breather must use exactly the correct fuel, such as kerosene. It should only light when sprayed into a fine mist. It must have the right balance of fuel and the gas **oxygen** to ignite. (Fire feeds on oxygen.)

Of course, all of this has to be done just right, and it takes training to use the proper technique, fuel, and safety judgment. A mistake could lead to serious injury—or even death.

Anytime a person uses fire in stunts, there are serious risks involved. People risk death or serious burns from accidentally lighting themselves on fire. Unpredictable winds can move fire toward the performer, or the performer might accidentally inhale the flames. Another concern is accidentally inhaling or swallowing the fuel, which is poisonous. There is also the long-term risk of **cancer**, painful sores called **ulcers**, and problems with the **respiratory system** (the parts of the body to do with breathing) from inhaling even small amounts of smoke over a long period of time.

Eating fire

Others daredevils prefer to "eat" fire. The practice of fire-eating originally came from India, where it was part of religious performances. Some fire-eaters put out flames in their mouths. Others transfer flames from place to place using their mouths. In 2008 a German man named Hubertus Wawra, also known as "Master of Hellfire," set a record by extinguishing 68 torches with his mouth in one minute.

If it seems as though putting a flame or flaming object in your mouth would be dangerous, that is because it is! Training in the proper techniques is necessary to do it safely. Even then, however, it requires pain endurance. Even professional fire-eaters get burns on their mouth and throat. It is a dangerous feat to perform, even with the proper training.

Fire-breathing is an exciting, dramatic spectacle. But professional fire-breathers are always taking a risk when practicing their art.

Snake charming

The practice of snake charming as we know it today came from India or Egypt, and it continued on as a sideshow tradition around the world. The snake charmer sits next to a covered basket or pot. The charmer then removes the lid and begins playing a flute-like instrument. The venomous (poisonous) snake eventually rises out from the container, as if drawn out by the charmer's music. The cobra is a popular choice for snake charmers.

A cruel trick

Snake charming is now a dying profession. One reason is the fact that it is often cruel for the snake. The snake is taken from its natural environment and kept in a small basket. Some charmers remove the snake's fangs or venom glands. Others even sew the snake's mouth shut, leaving only enough room for the tongue to flick in and out, to fool the audience.

Once people learned of this cruelty, snake charming lost its popularity and was restricted by law. However, thousands of snake charmers still practice in India even though shows featuring snakes have been banned.

SNAKE HANDLING

Snake handling, or serpent handling, is a religious **ritual** that started in the Appalachian Mountains of the southeastern United States in the early 1900s. People who follow this ritual reference a passage from the Christian Bible that says God's true believers will be willing to handle deadly serpents. Members of these churches say they are following God's will by making serpents part of their religious ceremony. They believe whatever happens to them is God's will. Many members of serpent-handling churches have scars from past bites, with crippled limbs or missing fingers, and others have died. Today, in states such as Kentucky, it is illegal to handle **reptiles** as a part of religious services.

SURVIVAL SCIENCE

The science behind snake charming

In snake charming, the snake is actually responding to the movements of the snake charmer and flute, rather than the sound. The snake rises up into its normal standing, defensive posture and spreads its hood. But snake charmers are not usually really in danger. They make sure to sit just out of striking range, which is no more than one-third of the snake's body length. Also, as previously mentioned, the snake often does not even have venom or the ability to hurt the snake charmer. The snake may also be reluctant to strike because it has learned the hard way that biting the solid flute will only cause it pain.

Early snake charmers were sometimes considered holy men and healers.

He could eat glass and metal, but Michel Lotito said hard-boiled eggs and bananas made him sick to his stomach!

Food daredevil

Strange as it may sound, some performers entertain audiences with daredevil eating! Frenchman Michel Lotito, also known as Monsieur Mangetout ("Mr. Eat Everything"), ate as much as 1 kilogram (2 pounds) of metal a day. To entertain crowds, Michel ate metal, glass, and rubber from things such as bicycles, televisions, and even a small airplane! Somehow he did not suffer from this diet. He died of natural causes in 2007.

EVERYDAY FOOD DAREDEVILS

- Everyday people can also be daredevils when they go out to eat. Fugu is a prized food in Japan. It is made from puffer fish, which contains a deadly poison in many of its organs. Chefs undergo years of training, because one mistake can kill a customer.

- In Sardinia, Italy, you can find a cheese called casu marzu. If the maggots in the cheese are still wriggling, the cheese is thought to be good to eat! If the maggots are not moving, the cheese is considered poisonous.

- Live octopus tentacles are a Korean specialty, served fresh and still wriggling. You have to chew it up well, however, or a sucker could stick to the back of your throat and suffocate you!

EATING RECORDS

Rather than eat dangerous foods, some people eat dangerous amounts of food in eating contests. Here are some records. (DON'T TRY THIS AT HOME):

NAME	RECORD	TIME	DATE
Sonya Thomas	65 hard-boiled eggs	6 min., 40 sec.	September 13, 2003
Joey Chestnut	47 grilled-cheese sandwiches	10 min.	June 10, 2006
Joey Chestnut	68 Nathan's Famous hot dogs and buns	10 min.	July 4, 2009
Sonya Thomas	46-dozen oysters	10 min.	March 20, 2005
Ken Edwards	36 Madagascar hissing cockroaches	1 min.	March 5, 2001
Takeru Kobayashi	8 kg (17.7 lb.) cow brains	15 min.	February 12, 2002
Dominic Cardo	1.5 kg (3.3 lb.) whole cow tongue	12 min.	February 21, 2002
Sonya Thomas	5 kg (11 lb.) cheesecake	9 min.	September 26, 2004
Eric Livingston	1.4 kg (3 lb.) haggis	8 min.	October 8, 2008
Oleg Zhornitskiy	3.6 kg (8 lb.) mayonnaise	8 min.	February 21, 2002

FANTASTIC MOVIE STUNTS

Some of the most commonly seen stunts involve movie magic. Stunt people have been creating amazing scenes in the movies for decades, while making sure actors stay safe. Sometimes stunts involve amazing jumps, fights, or crashes. Other times they involve fire and explosions.

The role of stunt people

Even though they take a lot of risks, stunt people make sure they are safe during the dangerous stunts they perform. They do a lot of physical training and research before a stunt. Many stunt people have a background in the circus. Some are athletes in sports like gymnastics, martial arts, motocross, and skateboarding.

Stunt people repeatedly practice the motions involved in their stunts before they are filmed. Major stunt sequences in movies are very expensive to film, so filmmakers want to make sure that no mistakes are made when the cameras are rolling. It is a lot easier, and cheaper, to explode and break things than it is to put them back together!

Stunt people also need to be able to act and look the part of a character. They are often a "double" for an actor who is not trained to perform the risky stunt, and so they have to become a seamless, believable part of the movie.

STUNT SCHOOL

The path to a career as a stunt person starts with strong physical conditioning. Other requirements include dealing well with physical danger and the ability to plan and pay attention to details. There are some places around the world that offer training for the stunt profession. The International Stunt School in Seattle, Washington, offers a training course in stunt work and an introduction to the profession.

This stunt person has jumped off of a balcony on a movie set in Italy. The actor he is replacing in this scene is Johnny Depp.

Free fall

Stunt people sometimes perform at amazing heights. They jump, fly, or fall to create a spectacular action scene. When filming a large fall, stunt people need to research angles, distances, and timing. They must also consider weather and wind speed. Stunt people need to be able to control the movements of their bodies while in the air, which requires skill and training.

With some of these stunts, there is only one chance to get it right. And the stakes are high. In 1979 a U.S. stuntman named Dar Robinson jumped 335 meters (1,100 feet) from the top of the CN Tower in Toronto, Canada, for the movie *Highpoint*. The **free fall** lasted six seconds. Dar's parachute opened only 91 meters (300 feet) above the ground. At that time, this was the highest leap performed by a stuntman.

SURVIVAL SCIENCE

How do stunt people live through fires?

Fire stunts are some of the most dangerous stunts in the movies. Only highly trained professionals attempt them, and only when safety experts and medics are there ready to help if something goes wrong.

During some fire stunts, stunt people can wear a fire suit made of a material that does not burn. Sometimes stunt people have to hold their breath. Other times they can use a respirator, which is something worn over the mouth and nose to help a person breathe near harmful smoke or gas.

When stunt people are set on fire, they need an **insulator** to prevent serious burns. An insulator is something that resists the flow of energy, such as heat. The insulator used for movie fire stunts is a special safety **gel**. With this gel, stunt people can be set on fire without being injured for several seconds. According to *Guinness World Records*, in 2004 U.S. stuntman Ted Batchelor set the record for the longest full-body burn, at 2 minutes, 38 seconds.

Safety and training are required for fire stunts, and movie professionals don't take chances.

Fight time

Fight scenes are a big part of stunt work. Stunt people find martial arts training useful when preparing for and performing fight scenes. Fights are usually **choreographed** (plotted out), rehearsed several times at slower speeds, and then finally filmed at full speed. Stunt people and actors need to know how to throw punches and kicks—and take them—without anyone getting hurt. Stunt people also need acting skills in order to look as though they are really being hit and hurt.

Depending on the demands of a film, actors may have to participate in fight scenes with stunt people or with other actors. A good actor will learn stage-fighting techniques that help create realistic fight scenes without putting anyone in danger.

Crashes

Stunt people are also often called upon to create car chases in movies. Before any car chase scenes are filmed, computer animation is used to plan and rehearse them. As we have seen with other aspects of stunts, filmmakers want to save money by planning ahead.

For the actual car stunts and crashes, stunt people do not simply crash cars. Instead, they use reinforced cars. This means the car's frame has been strengthened with steel and can withstand more stress. A roll cage is also added. This is a system of strong, metal bars surrounding the seating area of the car, which helps protect passengers if the car rolls over.

SURVIVAL SCIENCE

The science behind movie explosions

There is nothing like a big explosion to get the attention of a movie audience. An explosion is the **product** of a **chemical reaction**. Fuels called explosives react with **oxygen**. An explosion creates a huge amount of gas. This gas expands with a great deal of force, creating pressure. The pressure of an explosion creates a powerful force that can be used to blow things up.

Special effects artists need a special knowledge of chemistry. They need to know the kinds and quantities of chemicals and the proper methods to create explosives. Once they have the right explosives, they need something to start the chemical reaction. Usually this is heat. Of course, since we are talking about explosives, special effects artists do not want to be near the explosive to apply the heat! Instead, electricity is generated from a battery and sent from a distance using copper wire. Energy can change from one form to another. In this case, the electrical energy is changed into heat energy near the explosives and sets them off.

MIND OVER MATTER?

Perhaps you have heard the phrase "mind over matter." This refers to the idea that it is possible for the mind to conquer the physical limitations of the body, including pain. Many people have accomplished interesting feats that seem to support the idea that the mind can conquer matter. Of course, there is often more to this than meets the eye. Read on and decide for yourself.

Walking on fire

The practice of walking on hot coals, or "walking on fire," is a very impressive spectacle at first. It seems that barefoot people are able to walk across burning-hot coals without any pain or injury to their feet. How is this possible? Is it that, through mental concentration, people are able to conquer their pain and physical limitations? Some claim that this is the case. In some **rituals**, fire-walkers appear to enter a trance, which is a mental state between sleeping and waking.

But **skeptics** suggest that there is more to these stunts. For example, hot coals are usually covered with ash. Ash acts as an **insulator** and prevents the coals from conveying too much heat. Skeptics also point out that hot coals are often volcanic rock, which is full of small openings. Such rocks do not convey as much heat to the feet of the walkers, as long as they move quickly. Fire-walkers also often wet their feet a bit first, before walking on the hot coals. This trick can create an insulating layer of steam when feet hit the coals.

One thing is certain: people have burned their feet while attempting to walk on fire! Walking on coals is most definitely dangerous.

A Buddhist monk walks through flames and hot coals during a festival in Japan.

Bed of nails

The feat of lying on a bed of nails is another impressive display that appears to show mind conquering matter. However, there is also a trick to this stunt (see box below).

For this stunt in India, six volunteers were piled between double-sided nail beds. Then at the top, a karate instructor chopped a block of ice in half!

SURVIVAL SCIENCE

How do people lie on nails?

How do people lie on nails without getting hurt? By using a large number of nails, the body's weight is distributed among the many points. This way, no single nail pierces the skin. Even if more weight or pressure is applied on top of the person, it is distributed among all of the nail points, causing no harm. The most difficult part of the stunt is getting into and out of the position of lying on the bed.

Levitation: Amazing feat or magic trick?

Another feat often thought to be an example of mind over matter is levitation. This is when a person rises, or makes someone or something else rise, in the air. You may have seen a magician perform the trick with an assistant.

There are some cases in which witnesses claim to have seen people actually levitate. In 1936, in southern India, a British tea planter named P. T. Plunkett witnessed, and even photographed, a **yogi** named Subbayah Pullavar levitating horizontally above the ground. Plunkett was able to check out the space around the yogi and was convinced that the feat of levitation was real. Despite claims like this, most people believe levitation is merely an **illusion**.

Modern-day **illusionists** such as the Americans David Blaine and Criss Angel continue to amaze audiences with what appears to be levitation.

A woman in Peru appears to levitate in a public area during a performance. Could the illusion be real?

MAGLEV TRAINS

The possibility of a person being able to perform levitation with the mind may be slim, but magnetic levitation is certainly possible. Magnetically levitated trains, called maglev trains, levitate above a track using extremely strong opposing magnets. Because no parts are physically touching, the trains do not experience friction (parts rubbing against each other). This means they can go much faster, and parts will not wear out. A maglev train in Japan reached a record speed of 581 kilometers (361 miles) per hour on December 2, 2003. The world's fastest roller coasters also use this technology.

Martial arts masters

Buddhist warrior monks (religious men) of the Shaolin Temple of China are capable of amazing feats that seem to show mind conquering matter. These include balancing acts, breaking strong things with parts of the body, enduring hard and painful blows, and feats of strength and flexibility. The warrior monks also demonstrate grace and precision of movement while fighting with bare hands and feet, as well as with weapons. The martial arts that the Shaolin monks practice take years of dedication and training to master.

Shaolin monks use the repetition of complex movements—often copying different animals—to train the body and mind. They also practice breathing techniques that help them focus their energy, or what they call *qi* (pronounced "chee"). Through practice, martial artists are able to focus their *qi* in order to reinforce and protect their bodies. In this way, they are able to withstand things such as having boards broken over parts of the body and other amazing, and dangerous, feats.

Focusing his body and mind, a Shaolin warrior monk is able to lay the full weight of his body on top of metal spear points without hurting himself.

SURVIVAL SCIENCE

Using the body as a weapon

One popular martial arts display—practiced by the Shaolin monks and others—is breaking boards, bricks, and other objects with bare hands, feet, and other parts of the body. But how do people do this?

The stacks of boards or bricks are usually held up only by the ends, which allows them to crack down the center. Martial artists' hands and feet are also used to hitting things, so they are tough and move quickly. They know how to use a bone in their hand that is much stronger than concrete when used in the right way. BUT DON'T TRY THIS AT HOME! This feat takes speed and precise aim that only come with years of training.

A Polish karate practitioner breaks a stack of bricks down the middle.

Martial arts records

The following are some impressive martial arts records*:

RECORD	NUMBER	DATE	NAME
Most boards broken with head in 30 seconds	32	July 30, 2008	Kevin Shelley
Most bowls broken with one finger in one minute	102	April 30, 2009	Fan Weipeng
Most coconuts smashed in one minute with one hand	81	December 6, 2007	Muhamed Kahrimanovic
Most concrete blocks broken in one minute	888	January 9, 2009	Ali Bahçetepe
Most concrete blocks broken in single stack with head	7	July 3, 2008	Narve Laeret
Most martial arts kicks in one minute using one leg	210	July 13, 2009	Chloe Bruce
Most objects kicked off standing people's heads in one minute	43	August 12, 2009	Zara Phythian

*According to Guinness World Records 2010

AMAZING MIND POWERS

One area in which the mind seems to overcome matter is a process called **psychokinesis (PK)**. This refers to the ability of a person to use the mind to directly influence something—for example, to move an object with the mind.

In the 1970s, an Israeli man named Uri Geller became famous for his displays of psychokinetic abilities. His television performances included bending spoons and making watches run faster or stop or start. He also has described drawings he had not been shown and performed other feats. Uri has claimed his abilities are **paranormal** powers, meaning they are beyond the range of scientific explanation.

However, skeptics like James Randi say Uri is falsely passing off magic tricks as displays of paranormal powers. James has used stage magic to explain how all the tricks are done.

There are still believers on both sides, but one thing is sure: they are good tricks!

Parkour and free running

You have probably seen martial arts movies in which people jump unbelievable distances and heights, or even seem to be flying. Actors and stunt people use the assistance of wires in these scenes.

In reality, the closest thing to the appearance of superhuman jumping abilities comes in the practices of parkour and free running. The art of parkour has its history in military training techniques. Originally, parkour focused on using the human body to move from one place to another as efficiently, fluidly, and directly as possible. Today, free runners have built on parkour and added new moves such as flips and spins. They use the city and landscape around them to move in efficient—and often amazing—ways, seeming to fly from great heights without injury. But the secret behind parkour and free running isn't so much mind over matter as it is science (see box below).

SURVIVAL SCIENCE

How do free runners not get hurt?

How is it that free runners are not hurt by falling from such heights? With precise timing and technique, free runners are able to transfer something called kinetic energy (moving energy), into rotation, or the spinning of the body. An expert free runner jumps from an amazing height or distance and then tucks into a forward roll immediately upon landing. In this way, the kinetic energy of the jump—which would normally injure the body and its **joints**—is transferred into the energy of a forward roll. The body experiences only a fraction of the impact and is not harmed.

Free running has become a popular new sensation in many movies. This makes sense because free runners are amazing to watch!

FEATS OF DARING AND STRENGTH

Some amazing stunts and feats have to do with escaping from seemingly impossible situations. Escape artists often risk their own lives to stun audiences with ever-more dangerous stunts. Other stunts and feats are nothing short of incredible displays of human strength, skill, and endurance.

The escape artist

Hungarian-American daredevil Harry Houdini was one of the most famous **illusionists** and escape artists in history. He performed with his wife, Bess, in the 1890s, working on new tricks and developing his **showmanship**. They spent years practicing and perfecting his tricks.

Harry became an expert at escape stunts. He offered $100 (which was a very large amount of money at the time) to anyone who could produce handcuffs from which he could not escape. He never lost, and the handcuff bet drew more and more fans to his shows. When he traveled, he asked local authorities to restrain him. He then always escaped, to everyone's amazement. Over time, Harry's stunts became increasingly complex. He once had himself handcuffed, chained, put into a box, and dropped into the Hudson River. He managed to escape only minutes later.

How did he do it? Part of the answer is that he was a talented **contortionist** who had great control over every muscle in his body. He was even able to swallow and then regurgitate (throw up) a lock pick or key—one of the secrets to his elaborate escapes.

In his Water Torture Cell escape, Harry's hands and feet were bound. He was then lowered, upside-down, into a glass tank filled with water, which was then sealed.

The death of Harry Houdini

One day in 1926, some students visited Harry Houdini in his dressing room. One of them asked to test Harry's claim that he could withstand any blow to his body above the waist. (He was also known for his feats of strength.) Harry began to rise to allow the student to test him, but the student punched him before he had time to tighten his abdominal muscles.

Harry continued to perform, despite severe pain, chills, and fever. After completing several more shows, he finally agreed to go to the hospital. When doctors operated, they found that his appendix had burst, causing an infection. He never recovered, and died on October 31, 1926.

Harry Houdini as a young man, shown here bound in handcuffs and chains.

Harry Houdini's influence

Harry Houdini had a great influence on the performance of escapes, **illusions**, and tricks. Today's escape artists have the benefit of television to show off their stunts, something the great illusionist would have loved. In the decades following Houdini's death, many went on to try different, daring stunts. A U.S. woman named Dorothy Dietrich was filmed for television escaping from a straightjacket while hanging from a burning rope, 15 stories up—without a safety net! Dorothy was one of only five people to have done it, and the first woman to do so.

Televised stunts seem to get more and more amazing. In 1975 many television viewers watched Canadian-U.S. magician James Randi, known as "The Amazing Randi," escape from a straightjacket while dangling upside-down over Niagara Falls.

Then, in 1996, U.S. daredevil Robert Gallup performed one of the more amazing escapes in recent history, called the "Death Dive," live on television. He was handcuffed, chained, tied into a mailbag, and locked in a metal cage. The cage was then dropped from a transport plane 5,500 meters (18,000 feet) above the Mojave Desert in California, with a parachute secured to the outside of the cage! Traveling at 240 kilometers (150 miles) per hour, he managed to escape, reach his parachute, and use it to land safely.

Modern-day illusionists and performers like David Blaine and Criss Angel work in the tradition of Harry Houdini. They add a similar sense of showmanship to their own amazing tricks and feats.

Modern escape artist Robert Gallup, shown here (at left) after performing his Death Dive escape. For the trick he was handcuffed and chained to an underwater cage.

Escape and endurance records

The following are some impressive escape and endurance records:

RECORD	NUMBER	DATE	NAME
Fastest handcuff escape	1.66 sec.	June 6, 2009	Zdenek Bradac
Fastest underwater handcuff escape	10.66 sec.	September 9, 2009	Zdenek Bradac
Fastest escape from a straightjacket	18.8 sec.	September 17, 2007	Matt "The Knife" Cassiere
Fastest escape from a suitcase	7.04 sec.	May 31, 2008	Leslie Tipton
Longest time holding one's breath	17 min., 33 sec.	December 30, 2008	Tom Sietas

Feats of strength

People have pursued amazing feats of strength throughout history, and athletes are always trying for new records. Some people accomplish things that do not seem humanly possible.

In the 1800s, before there were official strength sports, "strongmen" displayed feats of strength. These included steel bending, chain breaking, and holding large amounts of weight overhead.

Today, there are strength competitions for both men and women. The World's Strongest Man and World's Strongest Woman World Championships are the two largest contests. Strength athletics competitions include carrying refrigerators, lifting rocks, walking while towing an 18-wheel truck, and even pulling 70-tonne (77-ton) airplanes. In 2008 an Austrian man named Franz Muellner held back a Ferrari sports car at full throttle for 13.84 seconds!

SUPERHUMAN STRENGTH?

The term *hysterical strength* refers to an example of extreme human strength that goes beyond what is thought to be humanly possible. In 1982 a U.S. woman named Angela Cavallo lifted a 1964 Chevrolet Impala, a large and heavy automobile, off of her son Tony. The 1.8-tonne (2-ton) car had fallen off the jacks Tony was using to hold the car up while he was working under it. Angela was able to lift one side of the car high enough and long enough for neighbors to replace the jacks and pull Tony out from under the car—a feat seeming to display superhuman strength.

The only examples of hysterical strength come from stories like this. The professional medical community does not officially recognize hysterical strength. The medical community does, however, recognize the effects of **adrenaline** on the body. Adrenaline makes the heart beat faster and briefly improves the body's ability to deal with a stressful situation. Adrenaline also increases the blood flow and **oxygen** to muscles and allows them to contract more than normal. This gives a person a sudden increase in strength.

Incredible feats of strength

The following are world records for feats of strength:

RECORD	NUMBER	DATE	NAME
Heaviest truck pulled by human arm	7,710 kg (16,997 lb.)	February 25, 2008	Reverend Kevin Fast
Heaviest weight sustained by the body	1,459 kg (3,216.5 lb.) (71 concrete blocks and 4 people)	January 30, 2009	Eduardo Armallo Lasaga
Heaviest weight balanced on the head	5,180.09 kg (11,420 lb.)	July 23, 2000	John Evans
Heaviest weight pulled with the eye sockets	411.65 kg (907 lb.)	April 25, 2009	Chayne Hultgren
Heaviest aircraft pulled	188.8 tonnes (208 tons)	September 17, 2009	Reverend Kevin Fast

Juha-Matti Rasanen, an athlete from Finland, competes in the World's Strongest Man competition.

Training for the records

Training to break records and win strength competitions involves building overall body strength in the gym. Strongmen and strongwomen develop explosive power and grip strength by training with the things that are lifted, carried, and thrown in strength competitions. This includes large, heavy tires, logs, stones, and refrigerators.

A training disaster

Training for these amazing feats of strength is not without danger. In 2008 Scottish strongman Darren McCarroll was flipping tractor tires as part of his training for a competition. In the process, he tore one of his biceps from the bone. He thought his career was over. However, Darren underwent an operation in which a dead man's **Achilles tendon**—a tendon from the back of the leg—was put into his arm. After an amazing recovery, he was again competing as a power lifter in 2010.

Not all amazing feats revolve around brute strength. This water skier is showing off an especially impressive stunt: barefoot, no-hands, mouth-gripped water skiing!

SURVIVAL SCIENCE

The science of strength training

People training for a strongman or strongwoman competition train differently than bodybuilders. They are more interested in getting the maximum strength and power out of the muscles they have than in growing them. This is why people in strength competitions are stronger than bodybuilders, even though bodybuilders sometimes look bigger and stronger.

Muscles are not the only parts that strengthen with use. A constant increase in the load and stress on bones will cause them to increase in **density**, which makes them stronger. So, strength training creates stronger bones as well as muscles. (People who practice martial arts also build greater bone density—and therefore strength—in the areas they use to strike hard surfaces like boards and bricks. See page 29.)

Athletes such as weight lifters work to increase their physical strength, rather than focusing on sculpting their muscles as bodybuilders do. Female weight lifters in particular gain huge amounts of power as they train, often without adding a large amount of visible muscle mass to their bodies.

SPORT OR STUNT?

When daredevils decide to push sports like skateboarding, swimming, rowing, diving, or motorcycle racing in new directions, they can achieve amazing new stunts and feats.

Something like skateboarding, for instance, is already considered an "extreme" sport. There is a natural rush of **adrenaline** when approaching a ramp. Some skateboarding feats are more stunts than sports. Danny Way holds the record for the longest skateboard ramp jump, at 24 meters (79 feet). He accomplished this at the X Games on August 8, 2004.

Here Danny Way can be seen performing another amazing skateboarding stunt. He is jumping over the Great Wall of China!

Swimming the Atlantic

Some amazing feats are tests of human endurance as well as strength.

The Atlantic Ocean is huge. There are dangers like sharks and storms. Few people would think of crossing it in anything but an airplane or a very large boat. Yet some people have dared to attempt to cross the Atlantic Ocean in more difficult ways.

After his father died of **cancer** in 1992, Frenchman Benoit Lecomte decided he wanted to do something to raise money for cancer research. He decided to swim across the Atlantic Ocean. With the help of experts, Benoit trained for two years to build his endurance. During that time, he swam and cycled three to five hours a day, six days a week. He finally set out on his journey on July 16, 1998, leaving from Massachusetts.

Benoit was accompanied on his journey by a support boat. The boat had something called an **electromagnetic field** that warded off sharks in a 7.6-meter (25-foot) radius. (Benoit did encounter other sea creatures, including sea turtles and dolphins.) He swam six to eight hours a day in two-hour intervals. He then rested on the boat. After 5,980 kilometers (3,716 miles) over 73 days, Benoit swam ashore in France, having swum across the Atlantic Ocean.

Benoit Lecomte, seen here before his amazing swim across the Atlantic Ocean.

EXTREME DIVING

Diving can also easily move from a sport to a stunt or feat. Professional divers often risk life and limb. For example, many divers have taken the dare to dive head-first from the 35-meter- (115-foot-) tall La Quebrada cliff in Acapulco, Mexico.

Huge cliffs outside of Acapulco, Mexico, offer beautiful views, and spectacular diving. Of course, cliff diving requires serious skill, not to mention bravery!

Rowing the Atlantic

On March 14, 2010, 22-year-old U.S. rower Katie Spotz landed in Guyana, South America. She had started her journey from Senegal, Africa, and it had taken her 70 days, 5 hours, and 22 minutes to travel across 4,534 kilometers (2,817 miles) of ocean. It also made her the youngest person to row across an ocean without help.

It was a difficult test of endurance. Katie suffered painful calluses and rashes from rowing eight to ten hours a day for so many days. She also faced 6-meter (20-foot) waves at points and was worried the boat might capsize (turn over). Katie said that sleeping was a problem while bobbing around on the waves in the middle of the Atlantic Ocean. Lack of rest made the feat that much more difficult.

Katie Spotz has said that a solo journey like her Atlantic crossing is a huge psychological challenge as well as a physical one. That's why she brought three iPods with her on the trip!

SURVIVAL SCIENCE

Extreme technology

Katie Spotz accomplished an amazing feat with her crossing of the Atlantic Ocean. In addition to her own amazing physical endurance, she benefited from the equipment on her boat, which was designed to withstand hurricanes and 15-meter (50-foot) waves. She had a satellite phone, a **Global Positioning System (GPS)** device, a machine to create drinking water out of salt water, solar panels and batteries for power, enough food to last 110 days, and a watertight sleeping cabin. Katie herself said that she would not go on a trip like that without all the safety gear and technology she had.

Water records

The following are some impressive records set by athletes in the water:

RECORD	NUMBER	DATE	NAME
Highest dive from a diving board	53.9 m (176 ft, 10 in.)	1987	Olivier Favre
Longest journey ever swum	5,265 km (3,272 mi.)	2007	Martin Strel
Greatest distance rowed in 24 hours (women's team)	229 km (142.29 mi.)	2003	Imke Ludwig, Judith Schulz, Sybille Roller
Greatest distance rowed in 24 hours (men's team)	263 km (163.42 mi.)	2003	Matthias Auer, Christian Klandt, Olaf Behrend
Fastest swim, long course 400 meters medley (female)	time: 4:29.45	2008 (Beijing Olympics)	Stephanie Rice
Fastest swim, long course 400 meters medley (male)	time: 4:03.84	2008 (Beijing Olympics)	Michael Phelps

A human spider?

Some people push the sport of rock climbing to extremes. For example, French rock climber Alain Robert is also an "**urban** climber" who has become famous for scaling skyscrapers. He uses only his hands, climbing shoes, and climbing chalk powder when doing this. Alain has been called "the Human Spider" as a result. He has climbed many famous buildings. One of his most difficult climbs was the 110-story Sears Tower, now called the Willis Tower, in Chicago in 1999. When he was near the top, a thick fog set in. It made the building wet and slippery. Slowly but surely, Alain made it to the top.

Authorities do not always give Alain permission to climb, and he is often arrested when he reaches the top of a skyscraper. His climbing attracts a crowd and is considered dangerous. Sometimes, however, he has permission and is even paid to climb. In 2003 he was paid to climb the 95-meter- (312-foot-) tall Lloyd's of London building to promote the first airing of the movie *Spider-Man* on British television.

Alain Robert stands high above Moscow, Russia, after successfully climbing one of the tallest buildings in the city.

EXTREME SKYDIVING

Skydiving is a sport that appeals to daredevils. Joseph Kittinger of the U.S. Air Force took part in something called Project Excelsior in 1959 and 1960. For this project, Joseph made several jumps at extremely high **altitude** (height) from a helium balloon. He wore a full **pressure suit** and had layers of clothing to protect him from the cold at high altitude. In one of his jumps, he set world records for the fastest speed by a human through the **atmosphere** (the layer of gases surrounding Earth) and the highest parachute jump.

Alain is aware of the dangers of what he does. He has suffered falls in his career. They left him with multiple fractures. He also now suffers from permanent vertigo, a feeling of dizziness and sickness often caused by problems with the nerves and structures of the inner ear. But Alain refuses to give up climbing and is looking forward to the next challenge.

"Climbing is my passion, my philosophy of life." —Alain Robert

Alain Robert in 2010, climbing a skyscraper in Paris, France. It only took him about 50 minutes to reach the top.

Pushing further: Machines

Machines add another level of possibility to amazing stunts and feats. Daredevils find ways to push sports and pastimes like motorcycle racing to incredible extremes.

Motorcycle stunts: Evel Knievel

Even though he often crashed, U.S. motorcyclist Evel Knievel became a popular motorcycle daredevil. On New Year's Eve 1967, he suffered a terrible crash while filming a jump over the fountains in front of Caesars Palace in Las Vegas. He broke many bones and had a concussion (head injury). Evel was in a coma (deep state of unconsciousness) for 29 days. His amazing crash made him famous.

But Evel continued to perform dangerous stunts. Another failed jump in 1974, over Snake River Canyon in Idaho, made him even more famous when he walked away with only minor injuries. Evel's motorcycle and star-spangled leather jumpsuit are now in the Smithsonian Institution in Washington, D.C., where he is honored as a legendary U.S. daredevil.

Continuing the tradition

Today, people like Australian stunt rider Robbie Maddison continue the tradition. He holds the record distance of 107 meters (350 feet) for a motorcycle jump. In 2009 he did a backflip over the Thames River in London on a motorcycle. And in 2010, he jumped over the 85-meter- (279-foot-) wide Corinth Canal in Greece. He was 91 meters (300 feet) above the canal's surface during the jump.

Robbie Maddison jumped his motorcycle across the Corinth Canal on April 8, 2010.

Humans and machines

The following are some impressive records set by people using machines:

RECORD	NUMBER	DATE	NAME
Farthest human-powered flight	115.11 km (71.52 mi.)	April 23, 1988	Kanellos Kanellopoulos
Highest glider flight	15,460 m (50,721 ft.)	August 29, 2006	Steve Fossett
Highest human flight using a rocket belt	46 m (152 ft.)	April 20, 2004	Eric Scott
Farthest distance on a snowmobile on water	69.28 km (43.04 mi.)	September 3, 2005	Kyle Nelson
Highest jump on a motorcycle	7.62 m (25 ft.)	January 21, 2001	Tommy Clowers

BARNSTORMING

In the 1920s, barnstorming became popular. In barnstorming, stunt pilots performed tricks in their airplanes. Sometimes they performed in a group called a flying circus. Some barnstormers performed by walking on top of the wings of planes and doing tricks while the pilot did the stunt flying. They had things to hook their feet under and hold onto, but it was still very dangerous. Sometimes they would even transfer from one plane to another in midair.

Stunt people still perform on airplanes today. This team is sword fighting in-flight at an air show in Cleveland in 2009.

SURVIVAL SUMMARY

Testing human limits

Some people attempt amazing stunts and feats that test the limits of what is possible and what the human body can accomplish and endure. The stunts and feats are often extremely dangerous, and some prove to be too much— people sometimes die attempting them. The stunts and feats you read about in this book were only possible with tremendous discipline, dedication, training, and preparation.

Like anything difficult and dangerous in life, surviving amazing stunts and feats requires a lot of hard work and planning. Even then, the danger is real and always present. Unnecessary risks and reckless behavior only lead to serious injury, or worse. Professional stunt people are well trained and prepared, and they always put safety first. See the chart below for a few more incredible records. But, for the nonprofessionals: DON'T TRY THESE STUNTS AND FEATS!

RECORD	NUMBER	DATE	NAME
Longest skateboard ramp jump	24 m (79 ft.)	August 8, 2004	Danny Way
Longest tightrope walk	3,465 m (11,368 ft.)	July 13, 1969	Henri Rochetain
Longest tightrope cycle	71.63 m (235 ft.)	October 15, 2008	Nik Wallenda
Farthest human cannonball flight	56.64 m (185 ft., 10 in.)	May 29, 1998	David Smith
Tallest building scaled (Taipei 101)	511.8 m (1,679 ft.)	December 25, 2004	Alain Robert

Preparing for success

STUNT FEAT	DANGERS	KEYS TO SUCCESS
Human cannonball	Compression of spine, blackouts, missing target distance	Practice and preparation
Martial arts feats	Broken bones, cuts, serious injury	Dedication and training of body, mind, and breathing techniques
Endurance feats (swimming, rowing, running, etc.)	Physical and mental exhaustion, dehydration, serious injury	Athletic training and preparation
Fire-breathing	Burns, fuel poisoning, **ulcers**, **cancer**, other serious injury, and death	Training and proper fuel and technique
Fire-eating	Serious burns to mouth and throat	Training and understanding of proper technique, and endurance of pain
Sword-swallowing	Serious internal injuries and death	Training, practice, and the ability to relax gag reflexes
Daredevil jumps	Serious injury and death	Training, practice, and judgment
Movie stunts	Serious burns, injury, and death	Athletic ability, training, practice, use of science and technology, such as an **insulator**
Walking on fire	Serious burns	Use of **porous** rock, insulating ash, water to cool the feet, and a quick pace while walking
Lying on bed of nails	Puncture wounds and serious injury	Use of a large number of nails to distribute the weight over many points and prevent the piercing of the skin
Snake charming	Snakebite causing serious injury or death	Often a cruel trick; staying just beyond striking distance and training the cobra that it is painful to strike the flute
Amazing escapes	Serious injury and death	Training and practice, flexibility, control of muscles, skill picking locks, ability to hold breath for large amounts of time
Feats of strength	Serious injury and death	Strength and endurance training of body's muscles and bone structure

GLOSSARY

Achilles tendon part of the body that connects the muscles in the back of the foot with the muscles of the lower leg

adrenaline chemical produced by the body when you are excited, afraid, or angry that makes your heart beat faster and briefly improves your body's ability to deal with a stressful situation

altitude height of something above the sea

atmosphere mixture of gases that surrounds the Earth

cancer serious disease in which cells in one part of the body start to grow in a way that harms the body, such as in tumors

chemical reaction natural process in which atoms of chemicals mix and rearrange themselves to form new substances

choreograph arrange how fighters or dancers should move during a scene or performance

contortionist someone who twists their body into strange positions to entertain people

density degree to which an area is filled in with something; relationship between the mass of something and its size

electromagnetic field field of force that results from an electric charge in motion, has both electric and magnetic parts, and contains a certain amount of electromagnetic energy

esophagus tube between the mouth and stomach down which food passes

free fall movement of someone or something through the air without engine power, such as the time before a parachute opens

gag reflex contraction of the muscles of the throat caused by the pharynx being touched

gel thick, wet substance, like jelly

illusion act that looks real but is not

illusionist someone who performs illusions

insulator material that does not allow heat, electricity, or sound to pass through it

joint part of your body that can bend because two bones meet there

oxygen gas present in air that has no color or smell and is necessary for most animals and plants to live; it is a chemical element with the symbol "O"

paranormal events that seem strange and mysterious and cannot be explained by science

porous allowing air or liquid to pass slowly through many very small holes

pressure suit airtight suit that can be inflated to maintain normal pressure on a person in space or at extremely high altitudes

product result of a natural or chemical process

psychokinesis (PK) moving of solid objects using only the power of the mind

reptile type of animal, such as a snake or lizard, that lays eggs and whose body temperature changes with the temperature around it

respiratory system system by which oxygen is taken into the body and exchanged with carbon dioxide; system to do with breathing

ritual ceremony performed in a certain way to mark an important occasion

showmanship skill at entertaining people and getting their attention

skeptic someone who doubts or disagrees with particular claims or statements generally thought to be true

sphincter muscle that surrounds an opening in the body and can become tight in order to close the opening

ulcer sore area on a person's skin or inside their body that may bleed or produce poisonous substances

urban relating to cities and towns (as opposed to the country)

yogi someone who has a lot of knowledge about yoga and can teach it to other people

FIND OUT MORE

IDEAS FOR RESEARCH

The sources in this section will help you do more research on amazing stunts and feats. Here are some questions you could consider when researching:

Now that you've read about some amazing stunts and feats, what do you think? Are the people who do these things daring, or simply crazy? Debate the question with classmates.

What do you think of walking on fire, levitation, and psychokinesis? Do you think these are just tricks and illusions, or could they be real? Can the human mind really overcome matter and do things that normally seem impossible? Do some more research and decide for yourself.

BOOKS

Allen, Judy. *Unexplained: An Encyclopedia of Curious Phenomena, Strange Superstitions, and Ancient Mysteries*. Boston, MA: Kingfisher, 2006.

Calkhoven, Laurie, and Ryan Herndon. *Guinness World Records: Fearless Feats*. New York, NY: Scholastic, 2006.

Cummins, Julie. Illustrated by Cheryl Harness. *Women Daredevils: Thrills, Chills, and Frills*. New York, NY: Dutton Children's Books, 2008.

Guinness World Records. *Guinness World Records 2010*. London, United Kingdom: Guinness World Records Limited, 2010.

Harrison, Paul. *Gravity-Defying Stunt Spectaculars* (*Extreme Adventures!* series). Mankato, MN: Capstone Press, 2010.

Jamestown Education. *Critical Reading Series: Daredevils*. Carlsbad, CA: Glencoe/McGraw-Hill, 2001.

McFarlane, Brian. *Daredevil Over Niagara*. Toronto, Ontario Canada: Key Porter Books, 2007.

O'Shei, Tim. *The World's Most Dangerous Stunts*. Mankato, MN: Capstone Press, 2006.

Phillips, Adam. *Fantastic Feats and Ridiculous Records*. Hauppauge, NY: Barron's Educational Series, 2009.

Ridley, Frances. *Stunt Pros*. New York, NY: Crabtree Publishing, 2009.

Ripley Publishing. *Ripley's Believe It or Not!: Expect The Unexpected*. Orlando, FL: Ripley Publishing, 2006.

Two-Can Editors. *Info Daredevils*. Minnetonka, MN: Two-Can Publishing, 2000.

Woodward, John, ed. *The Planet's Most Extreme – Daredevils*. San Diego, CA: Blackbirch Press, 2005.

DvDS

The Amazing Kreskin: Mental Marvels, Feats and Stunts. Kultur Video, 2005.

Hollywood's Greatest Stunts, Vol. 1–3. 1997; Montreal, Quebec Canada: Mandacy Entertainment, 2002.

Myths and Logic of Shaolin Kung Fu. San Francisco, CA: Tai Seng, 2003.

National Geographic—Through the Lens. Directed by Gretchen Jordon-Bastow. National Geographic Video, 2003.

Secrets to Survival. Starring Troy Hartman. Discovery Communications, 2008.

Stunts and Special Effects. 2005; Venice, CA: TMW Media Group, 2008.

WEBSITES

www.guinnessworldrecords.com

You can see more world records and stay up to date with new ones on this official website for Guinness World Records.

http://www.centennialofflight.gov/essay/Explorers_Record_Setters_and_Daredevils/barnstormers/EX12.htm

You can learn more about the history of flight and barnstorming, and find a list of further resources on the topic, from this website of the U.S. Centennial of Flight Commission.

http://www.niagaraparks.com/media/niagara-falls-stunting-history.html

You can learn more about stunts and feats performed at Niagara Falls from this website run by Niagara Parks, an agency of the Government of Ontario, Canada.